THE CAMPAIGN COACH'S CAMPAIGN BLUEPRINT

From Campaign Kickoff through Election Night and Beyond: The How-to Guide for Local Candidates

by Craig W. Turner – "The Campaign Coach"

Other Books by Craig W. Turner

Fiction

Wilton's Gold – Book 1: Fortune
Wilton's Gold – Book 2: Fulfillment
Wilton's Gold – Book 3: Fate
Border Troubles

Copyright © 2017 by Craig W. Turner
BMD Publishing. All Rights Reserved
BMDPublishing@marketdominationllc.com

ISBN #978-1544259666

Cover Photo: © Craig W. Turner
Cover Design: Kristin Watt

Printed in the United States of America

To Nadine
You know why

TABLE OF CONTENTS

WHAT MAKES YOU SO SPECIAL?

In creating The Campaign Coach program, I had to ask myself a question that I'm going to ask you to ask yourself many times: What makes me so special?

I put a great deal of time into understanding what differentiates me as a political consultant from others with similar expertise and experience. What did I have to offer that was worth people giving me their trust and accepting my guidance as they prepare to run for office?

I have been involved with enough campaigns to understand fully that people's motives for running, and the motives of those backing them, are not always about instituting good government. Maintaining political fiefdoms, drawing out votes for other candidates, political domination, eliminating opposition and a host of other reasons for running are too often a reality. As you read through this workbook, sign on to our webinars, watch our FAQ videos and go through the program, you'll see that while providing you the tools necessary to win a campaign is our priority, offering you the tools to also be an effective representative of the people whose votes you're getting is equally as high on our list. This isn't just about winning... It's about winning with purpose.

The truth is that despite (we hope) the best intentions of those serving, local governments in America are often poorly run. And at a time when educated, active and engaged voters are most needed, turnout across the country – particularly in local elections – is apathetic. As a result, elections are too often easily manipulated by special interests or political parties, leaving partisan governments filled with animosity and unable to collaborate and get things done. The combative spirit in Washington may be insurmountable, but there's no need for it to be that way at the local level. We all know of great stories in our communities where local officials were able to work together in the best interest of taxpayers. Unfortunately, we know about those stories because they're the exception, not the norm. It doesn't happen as much as it should or could. My hope is that candidates who go through The Campaign Coach program will not only be victorious, but will understand how government works, have a strong grasp of their role in it, and be ready to lead.

I trust that if you're reading this Blueprint, you have some level of interest in running for office, and if you've taken this step to engage, you have a purpose for running. Through this program, we're going to identify and highlight that purpose, and then put you in the best position to achieve it. That's what's so special about The Campaign Coach program. It's not just about running a campaign, and it's not even just about winning a campaign. It's about strengthening you both as a candidate and a public official.

This book is written from the perspective of you – because by purchasing it, you've become my client. We're not here to advance any political party agenda or help any political committee take over your town. I'm here to help you build the best foundation to run a winning campaign, and to be an effective leader in your community once in office. Understanding that running for the role of public servant has some degree of selflessness to it, read this guide from a selfish perspective. Because while many people may support you, and many people may even carry you, in your campaign, you're the one making the time, financial and political investment, and we want to make sure you get the return on that investment.

Craig W. Turner

"The Campaign Coach"

A NOTE ON SPECIAL SITUATIONS

The Campaign Coach program is going to give you the best information on how to run a successful campaign. Yes, some candidates will win from time to time because of special circumstances that make traditional grassroots campaigning unnecessary. There are more than 53,000 local jurisdictions in the United States, and we're focusing on the ones that are not anomalies – which more than likely includes yours! For those candidates who somehow end up with an easy road to election, our program will still be of value to prepare you to best serve your community.

THE OTHER QUESTIONS

Throughout this program, we'll be asking you lots of questions, mostly about yourself. Running for office is the epitome of putting yourself out there to the public. In order to do that, you need to know an awful lot about yourself, and the kind of person – and candidate – you want to present to your community. You will be open for personal and political attacks, and you will be asked questions that you would normally avoid. You will hear exceptionally good things about yourself that will be uplifting and often flattering, and you will hear exceptionally bad things about yourself that are both creatively constructed and potentially hurtful.

Obviously, if you've gotten this far, you're not taking the idea of running for office lightly, so with confidence you should be able to answer some questions...

Are you sure you really want to do this?

Have you considered everything that's involved?

Have you considered the toll it will take on your family?

Do you have a support network strong enough to see you through to the end?

What does winning mean to you?

What does losing mean to you?

At this point, these may be rhetorical questions, but you should take an initial stab at them anyway. Much of the information in this book will give you the various factors you should be considering. If you've already made the decision to run, and perhaps even have kicked off your campaign, answering these foundational questions will only serve to provide context for you now through Election Day. A deep understanding of your own purpose for wanting to be a community leader, a public servant and a representative of the people will solidify your message, strengthen your confidence and inspire voters.

Let's talk about what your campaign has in store for you...

ASKING FOR THINGS

For the next several months, you will be asking people for things – their vote, money, to share on social media, talk to their friends, media coverage, etc. You'd better get good at it.

Why have we chosen this to be the first point we make in the program? Because it's the center point of campaigning. If you have trouble asking for things, you're not alone. Whether it's part of people's personality or they simply haven't honed the skill. Asking for things on a professional level is an art that takes practice and technique. We often hear of people going into the sales field because they're good "people persons," and are great at getting meetings, working a room, and taking people to lunch, but flunk out of their jobs because they're not "closers." They can't – or aren't willing to – make that final ask, which is, of course, the critical one in their role. In many facets of life, if you aren't successful in closing the deal, the rest of the process is pointless.

Though it's not sales, *per se*, campaigning uses many of the same principles. Whether you're fundraising, looking for volunteers or getting votes out on Election Day, the path is the same as if you were in the private sector looking to land a new client – only you need to convince thousands of clients to make a purchase decision. Building relationships, collecting data, enunciating your value, and making "the ask" are all paramount to success.

One thing that makes it easier is to remember, as a candidate, that asking people for something is not an imposition, but actually a sign of respect – especially when it comes to voters. You can spend twenty minutes at someone's door and have a great conversation, but if by the time you leave you don't physically ask them for their vote, you've missed an important opportunity. It's human nature to enjoy and appreciate being needed, and if you can demonstrate that someone's support is needed to help you win the election so you can accomplish X, Y and Z on their behalf, and then ask them for that support, you'll tap into that most basic human desire to be needed.

Fortunately, most people who run for office have at least some degree of salesmanship and are comfortable talking to people (or else, what on Earth are you doing?!). Rather than being instructional, this is more about presenting the reality of what your interactions with people will look like over the next several months. It can be hard to get started, and count on it being tiring along the way. Like a good salesperson, train yourself to deal with "no," and learn to overcome objections. But we'll give you tips and guidance on how to do it, and you'll get better and better at it as time goes on, learning new tools and new methods for every conversation you have along the way.

"Folk who don't know why America is the Land of Promise should be here during an election campaign."

- Milton Berle

LOCAL POLITICAL COMMITTEES

Can you run and win an election without your local political committee? Yes, you can. But it's certainly much more of an uphill battle. Unless you already have excellent name recognition in your community and a team of volunteers, we'd be hard-pressed to recommend this course. Fully understand the challenge you face before engaging.

In addition to general campaign expertise, your local political committee can provide a wide array of resources that can be the difference between a successful campaign and a losing one. Your committee can provide people (volunteers), critical information such as voter enrollment and walk lists, polling and campaign funds.

Of course, running your candidacy through a local political committee is becoming part of a bigger team. Which means, even though you want to run there actually might not be room for you. Often, there are incumbency, an established "bench," heirs apparent, or other races in the community in your way, leaving you with a decision to make as to whether you build the relationships and wait your turn or force the issue today. Many candidates at the local level, if they're driven by something more than simply elected office (which I hope you are!), choose to take the more expedient path and run a primary or even change parties to look for an opening. Consequently, in some communities, the "bench" is weak enough that local parties run ads in the newspaper looking for candidates to run. Understanding your local political dynamic is critical, as you don't want to be blindsided once you've already started investing time, effort and political capital.

But there's a caveat there: if you're jostling to create an opportunity, don't put yourself in a position where (a) you can't win or (b) you don't want the job where the opening is. Many times, a local party will, in order to create bench strength, "find" somewhere for up-and-coming candidates to run. If you're interested in Town Council and driven to that seat with specific purpose, better to run a primary or wait the two years for another chance than sliding into a Town Clerk campaign that no one (including you) wants. You can derail your political career before it starts by running an unsuccessful campaign that doesn't even serve the purpose of forwarding your primary message.

But whether or not there's room for you is a reality you'll face early on in your campaign – even before you begin. For the purposes of this section, let's say your local party is accepting candidates and you believe it's the right time for you. How do you approach them to offer your intent?

Think of the process for what it really is – you're looking for a new job. You make the contact in the best way you possibly can. If it takes a cold call, do your research and find the right person – again, if you're to the point where you're running and have a chance of winning, you likely know some people. If you can get someone to make an introduction for you, even better. Generally, you'll be looking for the chair of the local committee, but there may be a "kingmaker" in the community as well, of whom you should be aware.

If your seat is contested at the committee level, which it very well may be, your campaign starts early, targeted to the members of your political committee. Committee members are a critical part of the election process, and have the final say who is going to run each year to represent their jurisdiction. Despite the influence that can be exerted on a committee, same as in any election, it's the committee's vote that chooses the candidate. You may need to campaign as strategically, using many of the same tactics, for your actual candidacy as you will for the election, itself.

Once you've earned the endorsement of your committee, the assistance it can lend you should have no bearing on how hard you have to work to win. If you're fortunate, you'll have a heavily-engaged committee that will assist you with manpower, campaign funding and expertise. But never take anything for granted. Remember that when Election Day is over, if you come up short, it will be you that wakes up the next morning alone wondering what more you could have done while your local party's committee members go back to their regular lives. Volunteers are volunteers.

That being the case, understand at the outset that this is a give-and-take relationship. Very quickly, your campaign will become your baby, and there will be decisions made by the party – related to your campaign or not – with which you may not agree. It is important to have an open conversation with party leaders prior to your campaign kicking off as to what they expect from you, what you can expect from them, and what the common goal is. You do not want to get to the end of October to find out the sole purpose of your candidacy was to draw out votes for a candidate in an encompassing district (or some other shenanigan!) when you thought otherwise.

NON-PARTISAN ELECTIONS – Your community may have a non-partisan election, which has its advantages and disadvantages. On the good side, there's no committee process to go through – if you want to run, you qualify and run. On the flip side, non-partisan elections offer some challenges as far as strategy, because without party affiliation, it's a little more challenging to identify your base voter. Plus, as we see often, the "free for all" nature of non-partisan elections can be unpredictable. Still, the grassroots approach to campaigning remains the same.

QUALIFYING FOR OFFICE (STATE-BY-STATE)

We have collected for you state-by-state rules for qualifying for office, which are available on our web site at www.thecampaigncoach.com/resources. There are different sets of rules in different states and jurisdictions around the country — petitions and endorsements and campaign committees, et al. — so utilize your local Board of Elections to begin and ask questions — that's what they're there for! Many local Boards of Elections offer a pamphlet or web page on "How to Become a Candidate," which will offer the most specific information for your community.

Note that there are often campaign finance rules that determine your status as a candidate, as well. In many cases, your official standing as a candidate begins when you create a campaign committee. We'll go into fundraising and campaign finance later in this guide.

A note on legal challenges — one of the most expedient

ways to win an election is to knock your opponent off the ballot before the campaign even begins. This is not easy to do, and usually means your opponent had invalid petitions or some kind of malfeasance in qualifying for office. Think hard before taking this route, as (1) attorneys to do this kind of work cost money; and (2) it sometimes can lead to bad press. There's something perceived as negative to the voting public related to having their choice, as Americans, taken away by the court and attorneys, no matter what the circumstances. Be sure it's worth the effort in the end.

Use the resources we've compiled. And if you need to collect petition signatures to qualify for the ballot, set your goal at double the number you need, to ensure that your opponents' lawyers aren't going to spend time weeding through your supporters' signatures to find issues.

Lean on your local committee and your local Board of Elections for guidance. It's both of those organizations' jobs to lead candidates along the right path.

"The best argument against democracy is a five-minute conversation with the average voter."

- Winston Churchill

UNDERSTAND THE OFFICE YOU'RE RUNNING FOR

One of the most critical early steps in your campaign is developing a good understanding of the relevant issues surrounding the office for which you're running — especially if you're running against an incumbent. If you give any indication that you're not knowledgeable on the issues or the governmental mechanism that you're hoping to be a part of, your opponent will use the slip up to demonstrate your amateur approach to the office. Remember that incumbents have a bully pulpit that you don't have, in that they're in front of a legislative meeting every couple weeks that is generally covered by the media. If you slip up, prepare yourself for seeing the phrase "Experience Matters" on all of your opponent's literature for the rest of the campaign.

In addition, knowing the issues of your office will help you to not get sidetracked in your discussions, whether in one-on-one conversations or at public events. Because you understand the role of a town board member doesn't mean that the people you're talking to do, and you will often have to bring the conversation back around to relevant topics. It is very rare that a local elected official will be required to take a position on topics such as national security, abortion or the gas tax, yet people will bring those things up to you. Be prepared to steer the conversation back to things that are relevant to your campaign – don't lose votes because of a position you take on an issue you can't possibly affect if you win.

On that note, part of running a campaign is making promises of what you'll do once elected. It is imperative that the agenda items you set during your campaign are doable from the seat. If your town is in the midst of a financial crisis, for example, people will find it not believable if you make empty claims that you'll restore cut services just because people like them, and your opponent will call you out on it. Don't promise to a disgruntled taxpayer that you'll put more snowplows on a state road that your town doesn't control. That's not to say that you can't educate the voter and let them know that you'll be an advocate for what they're asking (something you can do even before you're elected – see chapter 14, p. 39), but understand both the responsibilities and limitations of the office you're seeking.

We're big believers in candidates understanding the governmental process, which is why we supply anyone who purchases *The Campaign Coach's Complete Campaign Kit* a copy of *Robert's Rules of Order. Robert's Rules,* coupled with your city, town or village code, should be early weekend reading for you. We're willing to bet that you'll find holes in the way your current legislative body is doing business, passing resolutions or conducting public hearings that you can include in your talking points. Want to negate the "experience matters" slogan? Prove how ill-informed or ill-advised "experience" can be detrimental to your community.

Of course, the best way to get a firm understanding of what's going on in your local government is being active. While it may cause awkward moments, you need to attend council meetings, public hearings and informational sessions to get the pulse of your community. If you're running against an incumbent, be prepared for a lot of mundane business with a few obvious cheap political "pop" ploys – well-timed ribbon cuttings, grant awards from elected officials of higher office and same party, and perhaps the greatest and cheapest tool an incumbent has… The proclamation. A proclamation is a piece of paper that does nothing but "honor" people to get a photo in the newspaper. Believe us, once you get elected, you'll love the proclamation. Difficult themes will be off-the-table during the campaign, leaving you not only to bring them up, but to educate voters on why they're important. If the media brings a tough issue to life, it's a gift and use it wisely, because your opponents will hide from anything that's going to cause them to have to answer difficult questions (which is why in many municipalities across the country, the budget process takes place immediately after Election Day!).

Actual participation in public hearings while running for office can have positive and negative effects. On one hand, it's a bully pulpit and you can make a public statement to attract the attention of attendees and possibly the media. On the other, it can be viewed (and dismissed) strictly as a campaign ploy, and, unfortunately many times public hearings attract some pretty crazy people. It can be a critical error to a credible candidate to have her message melded in with public hearing "regulars." Speaking at a hearing is a decision to make thoughtfully, and perhaps in conjunction with your local committee, which may be able to also offer speakers supporting your point-of-view. If you choose to speak, you introduce yourself as a resident and taxpayer – not a candidate for office – and stay on topic. And regardless of whether you speak or not, if there's a public hearing happening, you should be attending.

Like understanding yourself, understanding the office will build a strong foundation for your message and will keep you focused on the realities of the job as you interact with voters. And, of course, it will make you a more effective public official once elected, with much less of a ramp-up period. Make your own education an early part of your campaign.

"An election is coming. Universal peace is declared, and the foxes have a sincere interest in prolonging the lives of the poultry."

- T.S. Eliot

FUNDRAISING AND FINANCIAL STUFF

Don't skip this section, even though you want to...

Running a campaign is about more than just shaking hands and kissing babies. To run a successful campaign, it will be absolutely necessary for you to raise funds, and then be an effective steward of those funds, donated by people who have put their trust in you.

Each state has its own rules about campaign finance which you'll have to follow. Early in your campaign it will be important (and in some states, mandatory) to recruit someone with experience in campaign finance to be your treasurer – someone your local committee can help you secure. With regulations covering contribution limits, expenditures, filing and record keeping, you'll need an experienced person to keep you on the up-and-up. Many of the campaign finance issues that arise (and the subsequent reactionary legislation to "fix" them) are actually not candidates engaging in dirty dealings, but campaigns without the right expertise to follow the rules.

Once you have a mechanism for taking in and spending campaign funds, you have to go out and get the money. The most difficult part of any campaign – particularly a local campaign – is asking people for money to ensure that you have sufficient funds to be successful. There are lots of things throughout a campaign that require money, and while you may have the best message or be the most charismatic speaker, if you don't have sufficient resources you won't be able to put your message or charisma in front of enough voters to win.

Like in any fundraising campaign, your budgetary goals will dictate the amount of funds you need to raise. There are many things on which to spend money in a campaign – printing, mail, phone banks, radio ads, palm cards, flyers, event down payments, etc., and knowing the particulars of your campaign plan will allow you to set fundraising goals.

Note: Don't forget about the importance of cash flow! If your campaign strategy calls for a strong mail push the week after Primary Day, you can't schedule your big fundraiser for mid-October. Understand when you'll need the resources for your campaign account and be up front with your financial supporters as to your needs and timing.

Fundraising is the painstaking piece of any campaign that candidates underestimate the importance of and have a hard time doing. In many ways, your background before you decided to run for office can have a tremendous impact on your willingness to fundraise, and your effectiveness in doing so. People who have asked for things in their former lives – salespeople, small business owners, not-for-profit executives, etc. – often can make the leap because their personalities (and their address books) in that regard have been developed. For many, it's an arduous task.

But that's the key – asking. You will rarely get the donation you don't ask for.

While fundraising events will be a key component of your fundraising campaign, don't relegate yourself to fundraising only through events. From the day you decide to run, you'll need to be on the phone working political, business and personal contacts for contributions to sustain the campaign. Remember that dedicating time to recruit one $2,500 donor yields the same result as bringing 50 people to your $50 cocktail party, without the costs and effort and everything else that goes along with putting together an event. While there are certainly benefits to building numbers, you can and should build your campaign treasury in large leaps with aggressive and effective off-event fundraising.

In a local campaign, the challenge is often even greater. In local elections, community members many times know each other. They go to the same church, their kids play on the same ball team and they shop at each other's small businesses. Which means there's a good chance that, even though you've known someone since kindergarten and they should rightfully be supporting your campaign, they probably have some kind of relationship with your opponent as well. And we're talking about people who can inject money into your campaign in a substantial way – not just people to buy a ticket to your cocktail party fundraiser. But there is often a roadblock in the form of a personal connection that is a deterrent to contributing.

In addition, at the local level, you'll also run up against professional relationships that cannot be jeopardized. Government contracts, permits, relatives who work for the town, advocacy efforts in progress, small business incentives and a host of other connections you've never even thought of can lead many of your closest contacts to tell you that, while they'll support you in the solitude of the voting booth, they can't do anything publicly. Is it dirty politics that people are made to feel that they are being held hostage like that? Probably. But it's the reality in government, and never underestimate what incumbents, especially, will do to hold onto their power.

So, now that there's nobody left to raise money from... How do you do it?

You ask, and ask again, and keep asking. Those people who fall into the categories above? Their honesty is a blessing to you. Ask them for their support, let them tell you no and why, and build your confidence as you put more and more asks out. But despite that type of pushback, there are some classifications of voter that do make viable targets for you:

(1) Friends and family – Of course, just as if you were starting a small business, the first place you look is to those closest to you. Friends and family contributions can be particularly beneficial early in the campaign, when you're trying to build a financial foundation for your candidacy. In the case of connections within your community that might be a concern for them, definitely play the "blood is thicker than water" card.

(2) Disenfranchised voters – Anger is a great tool for fundraising. If you're running and presenting yourself as an agent of change for your village/town/city, there's probably a good justification for it, and you're not the only one who's not happy. People, businesses and organizations who have been screwed by the current leadership are a great place to look for support. It's not generally the type of contributions you land with one call, but through building a relationship. When you've identified some good targets through word-of-mouth and research, it's worth investing some time to get them to understand your value as a candidate, and what you're going to do to right the wrongs that they've experienced.

(3) Influential friends – Among your supporters the hope is you'll have some people of influence in your community, who may be willing to reach out to others to solicit support for you. Often, this will take more than you simply being a great guy or gal, and will require some governmental (or political) purpose for like-minded people to rally around. But if you're that candidate that

can deliver on that purpose, asking others to help you corral more supporters of the cause is an outstanding fundraising tactic. What will you accomplish on these supporters' behalf once you're elected? That's the message.

(4) Organizations that support your platform – While there are many organizations in communities across the country that will offer endorsements but not cash, there are some that will provide financial support. When an organization offers you support in principle – and we're not talking about a "good government" club that made you fill out a questionnaire and go through a big endorsement process; we're talking about an organization whose mission puts them squarely in your camp and not your opponent's – it is important to ask what it means to your campaign. Invariably, the question will be asked, "What do you need?" There's no better opportunity to ask for a financial contribution. Come up with a number that makes sense for your campaign and for your understanding of the organization's capabilities. If they balk, ask for volunteers. If they balk at that, ask for press. Get something specific from an organization supporting you, otherwise the, support is worthless.

(5) Your address book – Reading this, your first reaction may be that you want to keep your professional and personal lives separate. We've heard it before. We've also heard losing candidates lamenting the day after Election Day how difficult it was to raise money. Your professional

relationships need to be considered fair game if your intent is to win. With discretion, of course. You don't want to irritate a client with requests for campaign cash, certainly, but if you're in business you likely have vendors who have an interest in keeping their business with you. If you're a teacher, it's a good bet there are other teachers who see things the way you do. As with any outreach, do it strategically, but don't write off your business contacts because of an imaginary rule you created.

(6)   Developers (both sides $$) – If there's one group that needs public officials more than anyone, it's the construction industry. Nothing in their world can get done without permits, variances, zoning approvals, incentives and all kinds of interactions with government. As a result, developers and companies in related fields are often generous campaign contributors. Of course, if you're able to land a contribution from a developer, unless there's a distinct pro-development vs. anti-development debate in your community, the likelihood is that they're also giving to your opponent. Which is fine. Your concern is not what your opponent is raising – it's what you can raise. Engage the development community and make a strong case with them that you can win.

OTHER PEOPLE YOU NEED FOR YOUR TEAM

You know, on TV and in the movies, when they show a candidate walking through her campaign office with dozens of volunteers and staff working diligently on laptops and securing votes on the phone? Well, it's probably not going to happen.

In an ideal world, you'd be able to create a robust campaign team made up of dedicated, hardworking volunteers – or, better yet, paid staff – representing various areas of expertise. But, as you'll find more often than not, local elections are not representative of the ideal world. That being said, in addition to your campaign treasurer as we discussed in the last chapter, here are some roles that it would be helpful for you to fill if you can.

CAMPAIGN MANAGER – A thankless and time-intensive job, the campaign manager's role is to keep you on-task throughout the campaign, organize volunteers, support fundraising, help with canvassing, manage events and polling, maintaining contacts and anything else that needs to be done on the campaign trail. In recruiting a campaign manager, focus on the word "manager." An effective campaign manager will have outstanding organizational skills. Since it's your campaign, you will often be tempted to take day-to-day matters into your own hands. Don't let it happen. Until Election Day, your job is courting voters and raising money. Everything else should be left to your campaign manager.

SCHEDULER – Your scheduler also must be a well-organized person, and can be a tremendous asset to any campaign. While this work is not as time-intensive as the campaign manager role, it can be critical to keeping you on-task. As a candidate, you will be pulled in many directions, for events, speaking engagements, living room coffees, lunches with donors and – since many local government jobs aren't necessarily full-time gigs – you probably will have to put some time into your day job, too! And you need someone proactively looking for the most important events in your community for you to be attending, too. Even if you can get a spouse or relative to help with this, the time that you're not spending on organizing your schedule can be much better used.

COMMUNICATIONS DIRECTOR – Securing a volunteer communications director for your campaign can be classified as a luxury at times. If you have the benefit of knowing someone who has relationships with the local media and can help with messaging and who is willing help is a huge benefit. If you can spare some campaign $$

to help persuade someone (don't overpay, though – you don't want to spend cash that can put your message into voters' hands on professional services), weigh the benefit of doing so. Between letters, press releases, speeches, social media, direct mail design and messaging, in general, a significant amount of your or someone else's time can end up being be spent on communications. If you can lighten that time load and engage some expertise, your overall campaign strategy will benefit. The Campaign Coach program offers a number of resources in this regard, as well, at www.thecampaigncoach.com.

VOLUNTEERS – We cannot overstate the importance of engaging volunteers for your campaign. There are many reasons why someone will get involved with a political campaign – from full support of your platform to the possibility of an appointment to a job or committee when you win. But more important than understanding why they're volunteering is understanding their strengths. If someone hates being on the phone, but enjoys door-to-door, you know where to use them. Miscast volunteers will short out and be, at best, ineffective, at worst, non-existent. Treat all volunteers with great respect and offer thanks freely and often. Buy a pizza every once in a while.

Local committee members are a different story – they've taken on a responsibility, and should be participating in various campaign activities. If they don't, you should lean on your local party chair for support. However, always bear in mind that they are still volunteers with other lives outside your campaign. Though they do have responsibilities, remember to appreciate them as respected volunteers dedicating their time and talents.

INFLUENTIAL FRIENDS – There are people in your community who will not contribute financially to your campaign for some reason or another, but can support you in other ways. Powerful and well-connected people on your side can introduce you to funders, community groups for speaking opportunities, and other supporters. This can be particularly important not only for your current campaign, but for future political aspirations.

Where do you find people to fill these roles if you don't have them in your own circles? Lean on your local committee to connect you with people with experience, and keep a strong database of people who tell you along the way that they "want to get involved" as a way of helping with your campaign. Call on those people when they're needed.

One of the fascinating things that you'll encounter is that all kinds of people will want to give you "advice." If you're new to campaigning, in many cases there will be those involved with the committee or your campaign who know a lot more than you do, so the advice can be invaluable. However, be sure to manage your time effectively. Advice can be given at committee meetings and public events as effectively as it can be given on a phone call or over coffee. Advice is rarely as valuable as volunteer work, and you'll learn quickly who are the real assets to your campaign, and who are the "talkers."

WHO ARE YOU AND WHY ARE YOU RUNNING?

These two questions define your candidacy, and they are critical to connecting with not only voters as your end goal, but with committee members for endorsement and volunteer support, funders and our own campaign team. People run for local office for many different reasons. Perhaps there are specific actions your current elected officials have taken that you feel have hurt the quality-of-life in your town. Or you have a genuine desire to take a leadership role in helping people that aren't currently being served. Your motives should be clearly understood, particularly by you, and clearly stated.

We've created this questionnaire on the next two pages not for public consumption, but for you to build an understanding of your own qualifications and purpose for holding public office. Out on the campaign trail, you need to be able to answer the "why" questions: Why someone should give your campaign money or time; why someone should give you their vote; and, in many cases, why your campaign should even inspire people leave their home on

Election Day to vote to make a change. Are you worth it? Answering these questions will help you to develop a message that you can deliver consistently and with passion.

To make this exercise easier, you can download an editable copy of these questions at www.thecampaigncoach.com/downloads.

WHY ARE YOU RUNNING?

What are your top selling points as a person as to why someone should support you for this office?

1.

2.

3.

What specific experience relevant to the office you're seeking do you have that will matter to voters?

1.

2.

3.

What specific experience relevant to your community do you have that will matter to voters?

1.

2.

3.

What are the primary components of your platform as a candidate?

1.

2.

3.

What is the primary reason you're running?

Who do you think you'll be able to help once in office that currently isn't being served?

1.

2.

3.

What is the first action you'll take once in office?

If they knew all about your campaign and your purpose for running, what groups would/should be your top supporters?

1.

2.

3.

What are your goals beyond this campaign?

It's important to note that some of these answers may change as you go through the campaign and learn more about both yourself and your community. But by going through this exercise early in your campaign, you will strengthen every interaction you have as you build momentum and engage funders, volunteers and voters.

"Hell, I never vote for anybody, I always vote against."

- W.C. Fields

IMPACT ON YOUR LIFE, YOUR JOB, YOUR FAMILY

There is no doubt about the fact that running a political campaign will have a tremendous impact on your life, your job and your family. It's something for which you, and especially your spouse or significant other, should be mentally and emotionally prepared.

A worthwhile exercise, early on as you're deciding whether or not to run, is to consider your run along two trains of thought: (1) what it will take to run the campaign, and (2) what it will take if voters hire you for the job. The commitment of each is substantial, and will change your life.

For both, it will be critical to have the support of your family, particularly your spouse. Running a campaign is one of the most time-consuming activities you will ever undertake in your life. You will be pushed nights, weekends and holidays with door-to-door campaigning, public events, fundraisers, parades, living room parties, coffees, and plenty of other items to fill your calendar.

Once you win, you'll have legislative meetings, community events, committees and people calling you at all hours of the day and night to let you know there's a pothole in front of their driveway that needs to be filled or their neighbor's music is too loud. You ready?

There is more to it than just the time, however. Running for office, you're putting yourself out there in the public domain for criticism and potentially personal attacks. While we all would wish that politics could be a little bit cleaner, unfortunately, they're not. You and your family should recognize the reality that people could say things about you in public, in the media, and in people's mailboxes that is anywhere between less-than-flattering and outright lies.

Involving your family in your campaign is a personal decision. Voters vote for many different reasons, and without question a photo of your family with your children if you have them will actually draw votes for you, regardless of your platform, your speeches or your visibility. However, many people, for valid personal reasons in the modern world, do not want to put their family's images out in public. It's a decision you'll have to make yourself.

A couple notes about negative campaigning against you... No matter how squeaky clean you are, there are things that can be used against you if your opponent's polling tells her that they need to attack. If it's not something in your past, then it's your inexperience. If it's not your inexperience, then it's something that showed up on your financial statements. If it's not that, then it's the fact that your platform aligns with someone else's who is unpopular with voters. They can and will find something.

All of the foundational work you've done throughout your campaign is the best defense against this. A strong relationship with a local reporter may get you a phone call to respond to "leaked" information. Having your voters primed to come out on Election Day can mitigate a November 1 hit piece that offers you no time to respond. Assume the worst and strengthen your foundation to protect yourself, your family, and your campaign.

We always ask our candidates early on what skeletons they may have in their closets that can be used against them, and then impress upon them that they will be used. Even if your opponent doesn't dig into your past, you'll be ready. Throughout your campaign, and especially at the end, we prep our candidates to anticipate that mail piece to drop, or that quote to be in the paper, and not only be mentally and emotionally prepared, but to have an answer ready. Understanding what can be used against you and why – and preparing both yourself and those close to you for it – is a critical strategy for your campaign.

WHO'S YOUR TARGET AUDIENCE?

Say you decide on April 1 that you're running for office, and let's assume you have no Primary opponent. That gives you seven months (assuming a November election – many states have elections at various times of year) to earn more votes than your opponent – a little over 200 days. The reality is, unless you're running in a sparsely populated town, that is not enough time to personally reach everyone to urge them to vote for you. You'll need to consider money in the same way that you consider time, too. Throughout your campaign, you'll need to optimize your expenditures of both time and money, focusing on two categories of voter:

1. People who vote reliably (known as "prime" voters), and
2. People who you know that if they vote, they will vote for you.

The philosophy is logical – invest our time and money into the "best bets," the people most likely to select your name on Election Day. Of course, you can't be exactly certain what people will do once they enter the booth, and there's no way of knowing how people have voted in the past (short of them telling you). But by analyzing the numbers from previous elections, you will be able to ascertain how many votes you'll need to win, where you can get those votes, and where you should focus your attention to secure as many of them as possible.

Targeting will help to advise your door-to-door, mail and phone strategies. For community events, private meetings, etc., you'll have to use your intuition and get advice from your party committee. Focus on where your votes are, and choose events that will get you the best return-on-investment for your time.

Many candidates feel that if they could just get in front of people, they could change their minds. There's a reason people major in Political Science in college, as opposed to Political Emotion. Barring extreme circumstances, the majority of the time it's the science that wins elections. Like it or not, voters are loyal to party lines, in support of issues that may or may not have anything to do with your campaign or your community. If you're a conservative Republican, the likelihood that you'll be able to switch over a life-long Democrat, no matter how aligned you are on some town issue, is slim. Don't waste your time on long shots. Focus on the best bets. Elections are a numbers game, and your job is to get more of your people out to vote than your opponent does.

There are exceptions to this rule, of course, and we'd refer to these as "issue" exceptions. If a specific neighborhood or the town little league or a fire district is having significant issues with the current leadership and your candidacy is offering remedies, by all means engage those audiences regardless of enrollment. Always remember that politics is all about "me" – if something affects my family, my home or my wallet, that's when I care most.

GRASSROOTS CAMPAIGN TACTICS

One area where your local political committee can be of significant help to you is in providing expertise and experience in understanding your voting community and their communication preferences. At the local level, outside of major metros, mass media is often overkill. Rather, it's the personal outreach, the building of a relationship through whatever means possible, that in the end will bring people out to vote for you.

Dictionary.com lists the definition of "grassroots" as: *the common or ordinary people, especially as contrasted with the leadership or elite of a political party, social organization, etc.; the rank and file*. Which paints a great picture of what needs to happen for you to win your local election. You need to be effective at making a connection with the rank and file voter, as success in grassroots campaigning will offer the strongest foundation for Election Day victory.

Of course, to do so you need to be able to offer something

to the rank and file voter that they can't get from your opponent. We'll define that as "value." Since value has a different meaning to different people and groups, it's up to you and your team to determine what exactly is the value that you offer. For your voters, it could be a policy change in your town, it could be money for park or road improvements or it could simply be someone who will listen – you will be amazed at how many voters you encounter feel disenfranchised by their local government (and pathetic voter turnout in local elections across the country is perfect evidence of that).

With that value you provide, trust is absolutely necessary. Don't grandstand. Every candidate in America wants to say they can lower taxes and increase services. If you have a plan to do so, then talk about it. Connect with your voters in a way that they're comfortable and can see value in you, while offering them something they can believe in.

How do you do it? Ideally, you would be able to sit down and talk with every one of your voters, but in most cases it's just not possible. Successful grassroots campaigning is making the best use of your time, your money and your volunteers. Let's look at the ways you can communicate with people on a grassroots level, and the investment you have to make to be successful.

Consider ROI when planning your door-to-door outreach. Again, you can't reach everyone, so strategize which neighborhoods have clusters of your voters that you can reach. Take a typical Tuesday night in July on the campaign. After you stop by your 6 p.m. event for an hour, you still have two hours of sunlight. Time walking (or driving) between houses is not talking with voters. If you can hit a walkable street where party enrollment tells you that you can access a bunch of your voters as opposed to a neighborhood where they're more spread out, you can visit 5-10 more houses. A few more houses per night throughout the length of the campaign can be an awful lot of voters.

Consider issues and hot topics, too, however, as you're planning your door-to-door strategy. If there are neighborhoods that have been neglected by the current leadership in your community – road repairs, zoning issues, pest control, whatever – those areas can be a great place to round up supporters in groups. Use powerful issues and people's venom for their local government to your advantage.

Part of any effective grassroots strategy is segmentation and targeted messaging. There are populations within your community that will respond to specific messages. While your entire community will not necessarily choose you on Election Day because you've denounced your opponent's cuts to the town's senior center, it can be a very effective message directly to seniors (who are typically active voters – why anyone in office would cut funding to the senior center is beyond us!). Take your pro-labor message to the union events, and your "cut the size of government" platform to business groups.

In your outreach, however, be genuine and follow through. In the sales world, it's said that it takes seven (7) "touches" before someone makes a purchase decision. Without a big budget, you're going to have to be creative to get seven touches with individual voters. But you can easily get two out of a door-to-door visit. Any time you canvass, you should carry with you two antiquated but essential tools – a notebook and pen. If a voter has a specific issue she cares enough about to discuss with you at her door or at an event, make a point of following up with them. Write it down, and then make a phone call on their behalf to the appropriate department, or connect them with others with the same issue. Show them what kind of public representative you'll be, and you will get a vote out of it.

"I probably enjoy campaigning more than most other people in public office because I like people and I enjoy going out there and telling people what I've done."

- Mayor Ed Koch

A NOTE ABOUT TACTICS

As we travel through this book, we are attempting to cover generalities that will provide a firm foundation for a campaign and, hopefully, a first term in office. Every campaign will have its idiosyncrasies, and different challenges to overcome, and your local committee will give you insight as to what tools will be most effective.

The easiest example of this is the difference between campaigning in urban, suburban and rural environments. In a densely-populated city, where voters may reside in apartment buildings that are likely not accessible, door-to-door canvassing is not an option, increasing the importance of direct mail and attendance at community events. In rural areas, you're not walking door-to-door, since homes aren't exactly right next to each other; if you're canvassing, you'd better be meticulously targeted. But you can access voters at community events and by being involved in local organizations. Suburban environments make canvassing easier, but if you don't target your walk strategy, you can spend a great deal of time talking with people who are never going to vote for you. Know your environment, and know what's going to work best to serve it – and your campaign.

STAYING ON MESSAGE

We've already talked about the importance of answering the questions "Who are you?" and "Why are you running?" The natural next question in that progression is the question that will be asked when the voter closes the curtain behind her (for the states that still use curtains – didn't it feel much more official than filling out bubbles like on a high school exam?)...

"Why should voters choose you?"

By the time Election Day rolls around, you will have made your best case for your candidacy. How effectively you've done so will have a definitive impact on your election results. Part of this relies on your ability to fundraise, your proficiency at grassroots politics, and how extensively you've put your message in front of people. But don't forget about the message. Because while many voters will support you because your name is next to the party line that they subscribe to, the strength and reliability of your message is what will ultimately capture those voters who are actually making a choice.

The key to campaign messaging is sticking to your overall platform, and steadfastly staying on that message. There will be plenty of things that pop up that will distract you, and the emotion of running a campaign – particularly when "everyone you talk to" is telling you how bad things are and how there needs to be a change – will pull you to engage with every single one of them. You can engage, but you must always bring everything back to the main points of your campaign.

For example, if one of the tenets of your campaign for office is fiscal accountability, and you're walking through a neighborhood where resident after resident is complaining that the potholes from last winter have not been fixed yet, the most effective message you can create will be to link the pressing needs of the residents (demonstrating that if elected you'll listen to residents' concerns unlike your opponent) to your platform... Saying "I'll fix that road if elected" is disingenuous, whether you mean it or not, and while it may help garner some votes in that neighborhood, it does very little in other parts of your town, where people may also be facing the same problem. What *does* need to be addressed is where there are issues with the current town budget, and why serious concerns as basic as safe travel to school, work and recreation are not at the forefront of the Board's priority list. Which is perfectly consistent with your position on fiscal accountability. Be the expert on your platform topics, and understand (and believe) how your areas of interest will help allay voters' concerns.

Many people throughout your campaign will want to control your conversation – your opponent, the media, and special interests among them. It is critical that you stick to your points, and always correlate the issues of your community with your platform. That consistency will be critical in those final days before Election Day when you're summing up your campaign to lure voters from their homes and into votes for you.

> **"It's useless to hold a person to anything he says while he's in love, drunk, or running for office."**
>
> **- Shirley MacLaine**

GETTING YOUR MESSAGE OUT

We're not going to sugar-coat things and tell you that getting your message out to your voters is easy. It's not. It's expensive and time-consuming and often a hit-or-miss proposition. Which makes it that much more important that your message is succinct, consistent and provides value. Here is an overview of some tools, and the advantages and the challenges of each:

MEDIA RELEASES AND PRESS CONFERENCES

Advantages: Third party coverage by the media offers validity to your message. If your opponent is an incumbent, she has a definitive media advantage over you in that every two weeks or so she's in a legislative meeting making decisions and taking action and getting coverage. If your positions and initiatives are of enough value that the media chooses to cover them even though as a candidate there is little you can formally do to enact change, then voters will respond to your ideas. Creating a community initiative around your message to draw the media's attention is a viable tactic, but beware of coming across as disingenuous – i.e. you wouldn't be doing this if you weren't running for office. An example would be suddenly seeking media coverage because you're running a program at the senior center threatened by funding cuts when you've never set foot in the facility before.

Challenges: The biggest challenge with media coverage is that it is not in your hands. You can put a great deal of time and effort into a press event to get zero coverage – and, if and when you do get coverage, there's a good chance the media will not only put their own spin on it but they may interview your opponent for her perspective, as well. Any successful campaign must have a media component, however, and in the next chapter we'll discuss how to make the most of your media interactions. As we've discussed, beginning a campaign with zero media relationships can be an uphill climb without getting someone involved who knows what they're doing.

DIRECT MAIL

Advantages: The greatest advantage to direct mail that no other medium can offer as reliably is targeting. Through direct mail you can put your information specifically into the hands of the voters you want to see it, which is critical in local elections where just hundreds, if not tens, if not single-digits, of votes often make the difference. We're not going to say that candidates can't win without a direct mail component, but it makes it very difficult without that direct outreach. If you've worked on campaigns in the past, you'll also be happy to know that gone are the days or folding, stuffing, licking and stamping parties. Most printers now have in-house mail services that are so sophisticated that you merely send your files and a check over and the next time you see your piece is in voters' mailboxes. Which gives you more time to knock on doors and fundraise!

Challenges: Cost is the toughest part of direct mail, because it involves significant fundraising and biting chunks out of your campaign account at a single time. With limited resources, knowing who and how to target your mail to is absolutely critical, and even then rarely are you going to be able to hit every mailbox you want to. Often, if you have a pool of strong financial backers, laying out for them the actual cost of your mail campaign(s) while asking for a contribution can be an effective tool – e.g. "We need $3,500 to send a piece to prime Democrats letting them know about the proposed move to privatize the Town's parks." In addition, with mail, while we all "know someone," it can be a challenge to identify someone who can design a professional piece for you at low cost (free is best!). For this, you can turn to your local party, or often your printer will have in-house design services that can be rolled into the cost of the printing and mailing.

In addition, the other challenge to mail is a combination of a shortening human attention span with low education voters. You may send the most articulate, attractive mail piece to voters, highlighting information that is critical to their very existence, that they'll glance at and pitch into (hopefully, for the Earth's sake) the recycling bin. That is an unfortunate and unavoidable fact, but those few seconds you get to spend with the voters you're specifically targeting are precious.

NEWSPAPER ADS

Advantages: Even though a political ad is a paid advertisement, there is validity to it because it's in a newspaper. This tool is very much regional, and you'll know best how your community likes to get its information. There are a few advantages to taking out a paid political ad in the local newspaper in communities where people swear by them, as it puts you square into the conversation. There's also the unspoken benefit of endearing you to the newspaper, itself – yes, yes, there's such a thing as journalistic integrity, but a newspaper is a business that has to sustain itself, too. You're not going to get a good story because you took out an ad, but you are going to enhance the relationship. There is also merit, if your campaign coffers allow it, to running time-sensitive ads for various events and milestones – Happy Labor Day Celebrating our Workers, or Congratulations to the Hillside High School Varsity Baseball Team for Capturing the State Championship. Good will goes a long way.

Challenges: Newspaper ads can be expensive, they can get lost, and you are never sure of who is reading them. When you speak with the sales rep, they'll be able to tell you how many copies of the paper are printed and distributed, to what neighborhoods, household income, ethnicity and all other kinds of demographic data. But they won't be able to tell you who's actually putting eyes on your advertisement. That's why coupons are such a big part of newspaper advertising – because it's a way to get some degree of analytics as to how effective your ad spend is. With on-line advertising and the wealth of data that can be obtained in that medium, there's some guessing when it comes to newspaper advertising. Know your community's habits in regards to local and regional newspapers when it comes to investing your campaign dollars.

RADIO/TV

Advantages: For many of you who will be reading this book, radio and television ads won't be a viable tool for getting your message out – either because their too expensive or the coverage area is just too widespread to reach a specific segment of voters. That being said, if you are in a market where it makes sense both from a spend and return-on-investment perspective, they can be a powerful medium. Why? Because you're spending your entire campaign trying to get people to invite you into their living rooms for one-on-one conversations, and radio and television give you the opportunity to do exactly that. There's a personification that you can't get in a mail piece, and, if orchestrated correctly for maximum impact, they don't rely on someone making the conscious choice to click on your posted video. If they're watching the program or sitting in traffic, they have to listen to your appeal. A well-done political ad can offer substantial validity to your candidacy, as well. In many cases, local media organizations can also be extremely helpful in creating an effective ad for you, as well, as part of your ad buy.

Challenges: While radio and television offer widespread reach, they don't offer the targeting that direct mail can get you. Close local elections are won by not only getting out the vote, but by getting out *your* vote. Remember with television and radio, in addition to paying for exposure to your voters, you're paying for exposure to people who won't or can't vote for you. Also remember that advertising firms make good money purchasing ad buys for clients because they know the strategies that make the most impact. Unless you have fairly vast resources and can afford some overspending, for local races you'd be better off spending your campaign resources in as targeted a way as possible.

SOCIAL MEDIA

Advantages: The advantages of social media are the same for political candidates as they are for any other kind of outreach – it's free (or fairly inexpensive, in the case of pushing or "boosting" posts) and can be very specifically targeted to people who are, or should be, interested in what you have to say. You have some degree of metrics on the information that you're putting out there, and a well-orchestrated campaign with quality content can provide as scientific a look at the effectiveness of your message as you can get. A full-blown social media campaign can be expensive, of course, but for the purpose of reaching voters at the local level, you shouldn't need to go overboard, as a fairly small investment on sites such as Facebook or Twitter can provide extensive reach in your community.

Challenges: The big challenge with any social media marketing is that the people you are trying to reach can choose to ignore you. In many other forms of media, you can get away with a message that is less-than-compelling to them personally, because you already have their attention, when the focus is name recognition. On social media, however, pushing yourself without worthy content will lead to people not only ignoring you, but potentially blocking you altogether. Remember, too, that the people who follow you across various social media platforms have chosen to do so. Getting them to share your information amongst a flood of information that they receive every day is asking a lot, so without spending money on pushing posts, your reach is generally limited to people who have already told you they support you by following.

SPEAKING OPPORTUNITIES

Advantages: Speaking opportunities are among the best forms of outreach in which a candidate can engage. First of all, you were invited to speak, so there is instant validity simply because the group that invited you put you up on the stage behind a podium. Second, it enables you to target your message to a greater number of people at the same time – that's political gold! There are generally opportunities to speak in candidates' forums at your local chamber or a regional good government group, but if you can get speaking opportunities throughout your campaign without your opponent standing next to you, you take full advantage of them.

Challenges: There is little downside to speaking opportunities beyond being asked a question that you're not prepared for. The other thing to consider is that there's a big difference between standing at someone's door chatting and standing before a roomful of people and enunciating your platform effectively. Public speaking is not embraced by everyone. In a way, if you're running for office you have at least some comfort level with being in front of people because it's going to happen, but the key word is "effectively." It takes practice. Perhaps you're a gifted speaker already and if so you should take advantage. But, for many candidates, learning to communicate in a public setting is a key component of their growth – and you will get better as you progress through the campaign.

A NOTE ON ABSENTEE MAILINGS

One important piece of your campaign that will require some time and money resources, but not a lot in a local race, are absentee mailings. Absentees are voters who are unable to physically go to the polls on Election Day, for health reasons, travel, military service, etc., and request a paper ballot that they will submit by mail. The beauty of absentees is that there's no guesswork for you as to whether or not they're going to vote – they have already proactively requested a ballot. Your job is to get your message in their mailbox the same day that they get their ballot, because it's usually a quick turnaround. Your local committee should be able to provide you a database daily starting a few weeks before the election (remember primaries, too!) as to when absentee ballots are being mailed. You'll need to be nimble to make sure that your mail pieces go out the same day. In local races that are often decided by a few votes, getting as many absentee votes as you can is an essential strategy.

As part of The Campaign Coach program, we offer these and other tools to help first-time local candidates create and implement a strong communications plan at www.thecampaigncoach.com.

MAKING THE MEDIA WORK FOR YOU

As mentioned throughout these chapters, the primary function of your communication and grassroots efforts to various audiences needs to be demonstrating the value you provide – as a worthwhile candidate for people to support and as a leader in office. What do funders, voters and supporters want, and how can you fulfill it for them? Well, the same principle stands for the media.

What does the media want? Same as any business wants. They want people to buy their product and visit their web sites. The media wants good stories that provide value to their readers/viewers. They want new information that can be investigated, and that leads to their "customers" having a reaction and engaging with them. Which is why sensationalism often rules the day when it comes to news coverage. Public relations professionals are able to consistently get coverage for their clients because they understand the dynamic and nurture their media relationships in this way.

As an announced and endorsed candidate, you have a tremendous opportunity to give the media exactly what they want, as your goals are very much aligned with theirs. Your purpose as a candidate is to differentiate yourself from your opponent by promoting new ideas and innovative tactics, and by pointing out issues that necessitate attention. If done in a thoughtful and persuasive way, this is good stuff for the media.

"Thoughtful" is a key concept here. Media outreach cannot be haphazard, and the media will not likely not give you coverage for weighing in on a topic just because you're the candidate.

* One asterisk to include here is that there are times where people have the good fortune of mounting a campaign where the local media already has a bad relationship with the incumbent or has already turned against her. In those cases, which happen rarely, but they do happen, the opportunities for media interaction multiply, and you should use it to your campaign's advantage.

Learn how your voters get their information from the media – if you're to the point where you are running for office in your community, you should probably have a good sense of the media lay-of-the-land. If the daily newspaper is powerful, but you know that everyone in town reads the local weekly rag, put some effort into building a relationship there. Reporters for weekly newspapers are frequently young journalists cutting their teeth in the business, and appreciate the opportunity to have the relationship and engage in campaign coverage. People, especially seniors, often have great loyalty to their local weekly paper.

How do you build the relationship? The same way you'd build any relationship – when you announce your campaign, reach out to the reporters covering the relevant beat and ask for an informal coffee meeting. If they accept, which they likely will, you'll have the opportunity to talk about your platform and your biography, and most importantly, you'll learn a little bit about the reporter's needs and tendencies. Though it might come, you're not looking for coverage from this meeting. Just relationship building. Do it, and it will go a long way. Of course, you'll want to put out a press release announcing your candidacy around the same time. Don't let a reporter's timing hinder you, but it's best if you can have any of these meetings directly leading up to your announcement.

Throughout the campaign, you'll want to then maintain a connection with your media contacts through a variety of channels. Press conferences/releases should be strategically timed and linked to your campaigns major tenets. When you make an outreach, pitch stories about issues that will provide value to the publication's readers. Make yourself a resource to the reporter by placing a phone call or e-mail at various times to touch base or share (credible) information.

Remember, these media relationships will carry over to your elected office if and when you win. The line of open communication will be a benefit to you in that role, as well.

PHOTOS FOR WEB SITE, DIRECT MAIL, ETC.

As we hope you're getting from all of this, voters vote for many different reasons. In a perfect world, I think we all would agree it would be best if people voted based on a good understanding of the issues with an outlook for the future. But that's just not the case. Unfortunately, people vote because of everything from the candidate's hair to the candidate glancing at their nametag instead of remembering them at an event. It's difficult to get into specifics because every person is different and different communities have different tendencies (e.g. a male candidate with facial hair plays well in some communities but is a campaign killer in others), but the underlying point is that a professional, relatable presentation is critical.

Now, as a public figure, consider yourself always being watched from the day you announce your candidacy. Maintaining a strong public image as you go about town is essential, and it's more than appearance — it's your presentation, confidence, posture, everything. You're asking voters to hire someone who will both lead them and be their representative. You must behave to fill both roles: assertive but empathetic, aggressive but inclusionary, and firm but compassionate. Instead of your everyday half-hour job interview, you're in the hot seat for six months.

Those characteristics must also be demonstrated in the photos that you use to present yourself in your campaign materials. The photos you choose to use can often be the difference between winning and losing a campaign, as crazy as that seems. Remember, when you send someone a flyer or hand them a card, there's a high probability they won't read a word on it. But they will look at the photos, and if the photos speak to them, they may engage further – or simply take their reaction to your photos into the voting booth. The photos must be sharp, professional, and tell a story.

Which means we're not talking about snapping some pics with your camera phone (while there's always the possibility you may come up with a good candid shot at some point in your campaign, you'll generally want scripted photos for use in your materials). If you have a volunteer who's talented at taking photos, outstanding. Otherwise, consider spending a few hundred bucks to hire a professional for a few hours. Get the photos done early in your campaign so you have them. Too many candidates scramble around at the last minute to try to get photos for their campaign pieces when it's crunch time – and often can't pull it together. Campaign materials without photos are worthless. Start early, and get these photos so you have them:

Formal headshot

Family photo

Photo talking with senior citizens

Photo talking with kids (must be approved by their parents for use)

Photo talking with voters at easily identifiable places in your community (e.g. Town Hall, park, etc.)

Photos talking with people at strategic locations that support your positions (e.g. union hall, business district, etc.)

Photo speaking at a podium (showing leadership)

Your graphic designer and/or printer will need these photos when they're building your campaign materials. Some quick tips:

(1) If you're knocking your photos out in one day, bring a few different shirts, outfits or ties with you so it doesn't look like you're taking all your photos in one day
(2) The photos are about you – not who you're talking with; perspective should be on your face
(3) Get advance permission to use children in any photos
(4) If you use outdoor photos, take another round of photos later in the campaign when the leaves start to change colors

(5) Tell a story: posed pictures with a bunch of people smiling at a camera do nothing; show yourself listening to voters, explaining the tenets of your campaign, and enjoying your community.

We discussed earlier the personal preference about using your own family photos on campaign pieces. While it's up to you, your family photo is perhaps the most relatable one you could possibly put on a mail piece or palm card. Consider the impact of doing so as you make that decision.

It used to be that a candidate would take these photos to use for their mail pieces and press packets, and that was about it. Today, with social media relying so heavily on imagery, every photo you capture can be used in an array of applications. Get them done early.

ENDORSEMENTS

There are a few kinds of endorsements that will be important to your campaign.

Party endorsements enable you to run as a candidate on a political party's line in an election. A party endorsement can be obtained through an action by the party or through a primary election. Either way, the party's endorsement of your candidacy means that the party committee responsible for the district or municipality where you're running is supportive (in principle, if not always in practice) of your candidacy.

In some states, such as our home state of New York, a candidate can be what's called "cross-endorsed," meaning she is able to run representing multiple party lines. For example, a Republican-endorsed candidate can also receive the endorsement of the Conservative and Independence parties, and appear on the ballot on three separate lines. In states where this practice, called "fusion voting," is allowed, multiple endorsements from parties can be a benefit for a number of reasons – including the ability to secure votes from voters who strictly vote their party line, and attracting voters from the "other" major party line who refuse to vote for your party's candidate (e.g. Democrats who would never vote for a Republican can vote for a Republican candidate, but on a different line to feel as though she's not abandoning her principles).

There are different rules state-by-state for securing endorsements, which we've compiled for you at www.thecampaigncoach.com/ resources.

The other kind of endorsements are related to public acknowledgement of support for your candidacy by influential people and organizations. Public endorsements, if you can get them, are an extremely effective tool, particularly for your communications program. In addition, these endorsements can bring blocks of voters into your camp if announced and publicized properly.

While influential people can often give endorsements, those generally come less as an announcement and more in the form of a small, intimate fundraiser in their homes. These are specifically effective for fundraising, as the type of people whose endorsements you would want to have are connected to similar people for whom you winning the campaign is in their best interests – now or in the future. The exception would be endorsements from other elected officials, which can be very powerful when they're not obvious (e.g. bigger-name Democrat supporting the Democrat in the race).

Organizational endorsements can add a significant boost to your campaign. They often result in media coverage if the endorsement is a significant one, and once you have an endorsement it's yours to use on your web site and campaign materials. There are many voters who will automatically vote for a candidate if they see that an organization they support is supportive of you. Of course, endorsements that come with money are even better. It's critical, though, to activate an endorsement if you want to derive any benefit from it. Getting a letter in the mail that you've received an endorsement feels good, but it's important to ask the endorsing body how they'll put the endorsement to work. Will they do a mailing or send an e-mail to their members? Will they craft a press release or offer a quote for your own? If a group is supporting you, be sure to ask them what their endorsement actually means. Often, you'll find out they don't know, and are open to your recommendations.

Be aware that not all endorsements – party or organizational – are right for your campaign, and be sensitive to your campaign platforms and the voters you're trying to reach. While you may be able to secure an endorsement from the local chamber of commerce, for example, if your constituency has issues with some of the chamber's positions it could actually be a negative. Remember that organizations making endorsements are also doing so to help fulfill their own mission. Which means that their reasons for endorsing you could be many – including the ability to raise money for their own political action committee by saying, "100% of our endorsed candidates won last year," or sending a message to the incumbent to prep for an upcoming event in the next term, such as contract negotiations or road funding. It is alright to politely decline an endorsement if the organization offering it doesn't have a sufficient level of alignment with your platform.

How do you solicit endorsements? Same as any other audience in your campaign – strong relationship building and demonstrating that your platform will provide value for them once you're elected to office. It's a good idea early in your campaign to do some research on which organizations in your community historically will make endorsements, so you can prepare and reach out. It's not a good feeling to see in the newspaper that your opponent received an endorsement you didn't even know existed!

ATTACK ADS VS. ISSUE CAMPAIGNING

"Negative campaigning" or "going negative" is a subject that comes up in nearly every campaign – especially challenger campaigns, where it is absolutely essential to differentiate between you and the incumbent to get people to choose change. Candidates, themselves, have very mixed opinions on the strategy, most prominently when they're starting out their campaign. They may wholeheartedly want to run a "clean campaign," or be at the other end of the spectrum where they have juicy dirt on their opponent and can't wait to run to the media with it.

Either way, by the time they end up in the thick of the campaign they usually find themselves somewhere in the middle. The term "going negative" is really a misnomer. Highlighting the differences between you and your opponent is critical to a winning campaign, whether it's related to your platform, your experience, your morals, or your ability to deliver.

It's how you do it that is important.

Despite what you may believe as a result of national campaigns, personal attacks are seldom seem by voters as a good thing. In fact, they often have the opposite effect, which is to make you look like your campaign is desperate. Yes, you may have significant juice on your opponent that you imagine if the voters only knew about they'd cast him out of office without even making it to the election. But it's not quite so simple, if it's obvious or perceived that you're the one doing the finger-pointing.

Tying the message into the public servant/representative of the people/caretaker of our taxes theme is the way to make it work, but it has to be done strategically, and in a way that makes sense. This isn't the time for spin and a bad segue that only you and your inside folks understand. There is always inside baseball that is important to you and your inner circle that the rest of the community has no time for or interest in. Learn to separate yourself from that. Whatever you make public must be relevant to the campaign. If your opponent made a legitimate deal with her private business where someone else unfortunately was screwed, that's hard to connect. But if your opponent had town workers pave his driveway, or if he was three years delinquent on his property taxes – then, you have something that pertains to people's trust of that person in the role they're electing him for. That can be used.

The catch is that you can't be the one revealing the information. Because two things will happen: (1) you will then be called upon to justify what you said; and (2) you may or may not have all the facts and what you're actually then doing is giving the media a reason to go talk with your opponent, and a free opportunity to defend himself. Don't do that. The additional risk is that the media (and potentially voters) will not feel as passionate about your opponent's misdeeds as you are, and your message will end up being hollow. In fact, the downside is that you've put time, energy and possibly campaign resources into NOT talking about your own message. Remember the importance of contrasting the effective leader you'll be against your opponent's weaknesses.

Of course, if the local media gets hold of some less-than-flattering news on your opponent and runs with it, all the better for you. When you're asked about it, which you will be, acknowledge that it's out there and, as we continue to assert, turn the conversation right back to your own campaign talking points.

Negative issue campaigning is often confused with "attack ads" or "going negative." In a challenger/incumbent race, the best thing you have going for you to differentiate yourself is your opponent's voting record. You're running for a reason, and most likely that reason has something to do with your opponent's actions while in office. Just because you say something about your opponent, it doesn't mean that you've "gone negative." Talking about your opponent's three divorces? Yes, that's going negative. Highlighting a voting record that doesn't reflect the interests of the constituents he's representing? You should be doing that all day, every day.

Don't fall into the trap of letting your opponent's misbehavior distract you from your campaign — and people will come out of the woodwork with terrible stories of malfeasance to "help" you. But also don't fall into the trap of thinking you're going to spend the entire campaign talking about your own platform and never mentioning your opponent. Attack strategically, and contrast with purpose.

EFFECTIVE COMMUNICATION/ CONNECTING WITH THE VOTER

This is going to be difficult for you to believe and accept: the words coming out of your mouth are not the #1 priority on the minds of voters. You've likely surrounded yourself will people who will make you feel that way, of course, but for voters, who just finished a 10-hour workday and the day care called and Billy pushed another kid at school and the gutters need to be repaired and you need to pick up milk on the way home, there are a lot of priorities that come before reading your postcards, reading your Facebook posts, or standing in the doorway chatting with you.

The point in this is that your message – no matter how it's delivered – must be succinct, and it must be relevant. This is the Information Age, and people are peppered with information from every angle. In many cases that information is coming from sources from which they have already voluntarily elected to receive information. Which means that people's attention spans are shrinking, especially when it comes to information they didn't request. Put yourself in the voter's shoes – how do you react when you get a mail piece, a voicemail, or a visit that you didn't seek out? Consider that when making your own outreaches.

If you have enough guaranteed people who support you and will carry you to victory, then more power to you. But for most campaigns, you do need to woo some people who have never heard of you, and some who are on the fence as to supporting you or not. And you still need to impress upon them to leave their home and visit the polls on Election Day.

The key to communicating with those groups of people is to create a message that stands out, can be absorbed quickly, and that speaks directly to their needs. Some critical steps for doing that:

(1) *Educate yourself on the top issues of the people you're approaching* – by neighborhood, by street, by school district, etc. Through media research, and certainly during door-to-door campaigning, it should become clear quickly to you what the issues of the area are. The closer you are able to hit home with each individual voter, the more you'll grab their interest.

(2) *Be clear.* Estimate safely that when a voter picks up your mail piece you have at most five seconds to get your name and a quick message in front of them. You'll often see campaign literature have a tagline such as, "Experience that we need" or "Dedication. Integrity.

Results." While there are those higher-information voters who actually will care what you have to say, for many the five seconds you get with them will be all you get throughout the campaign. Make it productive.

(3) **Be concise.** Soapbox speeches do not win elections. Too many candidates have their own idea for the community that is relevant to no one but themselves, and spend their campaign trying to convince people that... flowerpots along Main Street are the key to happiness for town residents (Yes, we've heard that). Keep your talking points on target, learn to be a better listener, and keep voters engaged by making your conversation reflective of their interests.

It's been suggested many times throughout this book that running for office can do a number on your psyche. You are surrounded on a daily basis with people who tell you you're going to win and the other guy is a jerk, and that you should run for U.S. Senate next. Never forget that you're running to be a representative of the people. Bring your ideas, your drive and your inspiration, but always remember that if and when you win, it's your constituents' best interests that need to be at the forefront of your agenda.

Once you've made a connection, and voters begin to identify with your issues and see you as a leader fighting for their interests and not just your own, is when you build momentum. People who are confident that you're working on their behalf are the ones who will request lawn signs, host coffee meetings in their living room, and get their friends out to vote. Focusing on making that connection will pay incredible dividends.

"I was friends with President Ronald Reagan and he once said to me, 'I don't know how anybody can serve in public office without being an actor.'"

- Warren Beatty

POLLING

It's a simple concept that the better you know your constituents, the more effective you can relate to them. There are several reasons you might want to poll voters at points during your campaign, but all are related to getting a better sense of what's on the minds of residents in your community.

Polling, however, is expensive – especially for a local candidate's budget. Depending on what part of the country you're in, these polls can run anywhere from $2,000-$5,000 for a local campaign. Weigh this expenditure carefully, as that amount of money could be used later in the campaign for a targeted mail piece.

But don't talk yourself out of it yet, because there are ways to get it done, and the results can be very useful:

(1) You know where you stand with voters – If you're early enough in the campaign, you could actually use this information to help you make the decision to run or not. An early poll could tell you if you're facing an

insurmountable challenge, or encourage you that victory is actually a possibility. Which is often important as you...

(2) Use the positive information in your poll to convince funders that your campaign is viable and your election is within reach. As in any pursuit in life, no one wants to back the losing horse. If you've secured data via polling demonstrating that your candidacy is legitimate and that your chances of standing victorious on election night are real, it's going to be that much easier for you to raise funds.

(3) You can get a better understanding of the issues on the minds of your constituents in a scientific way. While it's true that you will learn more and more about your community with every person you talk to, a poll can offer you insights and analysis of trends that word-of-mouth will take you most of your summer to acquire. You may find that a pet issue of yours is not registering on voters' radar, or that some issue that has been bubbling up will ultimately be enough to get them to the polls on Election Day.

So how do you get this valuable information having not yet raised any money, or without taking a chunk out of your early campaign account?

One avenue is lumping into someone else's poll. Provided you're running with a local party's blessing (and not mounting a primary), collaboration with other candidates in the field running for different offices that touch your community can be an important arrow in your quiver. If a like-minded candidate is running for a higher office – particularly an office that wholly encompasses your community – there's a chance they might be doing a poll that you can benefit from, either directly or indirectly. If that's the case, ask your local party to help coordinate. You may be allowed to put a question or two in the poll, or have your name added to determine name recognition. If not (remember, they're paying for the poll and many polls include a limited number of questions), if they're willing to share the information with you it can be as valuable as if you'd done the poll yourself – particularly when it comes to issues.

So let's say that doesn't work, and your own campaign is on a shoestring budget. How else can you get the information that will guide you through the election?

Just ask.

While it's not as scientific as a professional poll, a local candidate can garner some information on his own through a number of channels, including a door-to-door survey, talking with people at events and, of course, social media. They key is to not forget the science in political science. Which means that if you're attempting to do a poll, you must approach it as though you're doing a poll. Don't rely on the fact that one house or one street was strong for a certain issue, which is a trap into which many candidates fall. Seek out a diverse pool of people to interview on the same topics – similar to how a paid poll would look.

One caveat with social media is to remember that, especially with Facebook, the people who you are communicating with are people that have chosen to follow you. Which means that in many cases their answers will be biased in your direction. Don't dismiss the tool, but also make sure that if you're informally polling through social media, you're also using other methods to get information from people who aren't already backing your candidacy. The "Like" button is way too easy to misinterpret.

Once you've collected the information, and having spoken to enough people that you feel comfortable it's reliable, I emphasize again to regard it the same way a professional pollster would. What is this information telling me about how people are going to vote on Election Day? How can I integrate the message voters gave me answering these questions into the messaging for my campaign? What issues are they passionate enough about that they're going to make a point of voting in this election?

They call it political science for a reason. This is the Information Age, and decisions are made in all sectors based on data. If you're committed to spending at least most of a year in this endeavor, do it with the backing of information that you can use to make smart, strategic decisions.

GOOD CANDIDATES MAKE GOOD ELECTED OFFICIALS

All throughout this book, we've talked about the value of being an educated and informed candidate. Throughout your campaign, you'll probably have the opportunity to stay more up-to-date on issues in your community than you ever have before, with access to many more people and much more insight than you normally do. The more people you talk to, understanding that they will hopefully be your constituents and you, as their representative, will be speaking on their behalf, will make you a more effective public official once you're elected.

"Effective" is an interesting description of an elected official, because it offers a wide range of interpretation as to its meaning. From the perspective of "special interests" who may put money or other resources into your campaign, successful advancement of their specific agenda is the hallmark of effectiveness. From the perspective of good government clubs, it is likely your ability to collaborate and find solutions. The active voter may just want you to "get something done," and the casual voter may judge your ability to lead by whether or not the pothole at the end of her road is filled.

Whatever your interpretation is of what an "effective" public official is, a firm understanding of how government – particularly the job you're running for – is critical, and will benefit you not only once you're in office to implement your agenda, but on the campaign trail, as well. You must understand the inner workings of the body of government you're running for – how local laws and resolutions are brought to the floor, vetted and approved; how tax receipts are collected; where your town handles operations internally and where it works with contractors – and who those contractors are; how (and when) the budget process takes place, who the various department heads are and how they operate, and so on and so on.

We've talked about the six-month job interview. Would you go in to talk to a prospective new boss without knowing anything about the job for which you were applying? Get to know the job, then show voters, i.e. the boss, that you're ready for it.

Learn the legislative process. While you'll seldom have the opportunity to raise it during your campaign, it could come up. Be in-the-know on *Robert's Rules of Order* so you can speak intelligibly to voters or the media. When you win, you will be able to hit the ground running and be impactful immediately.

Door-to-door campaigning is so valuable not only to your election, but to your term in office. The relationships you've built and information you've gathered while walking neighborhoods for votes will enable you to best serve your constituents. Which will not only help to fulfill your original purpose we discussed at the beginning of this book, but doesn't hurt your re-election effort, either!

"In politics, we presume that everyone who knows how to get votes knows how to administer a city or a state. When we are ill... We do not ask for the handsomest physician, or the most eloquent one."

- Plato

ANYTHING CAN HAPPEN

With all of the advice we've given, the foundation we've helped you build, and the best of intentions, it's important to understand that in politics, anything can happen. It is inherently possible for you to have the election won the night before Election Day, and something happens that keeps your voters home the next morning.

As the author of this book and founder of The Campaign Coach, I have experienced this first-hand. My first campaign – the first one I'd ever worked on – was a county legislature Primary Election in Western New York, scheduled for September 11, 2001. I was the communications director on a number of campaigns that year, working directly for the local Republican Party, and we felt very confident with our chances to flip a majority in the legislature. After just about two hours of voting had taken place, we were prepping to kick off phone banks to get afternoon voters to the polls. Around 9 a.m., though, we learned that there had been an attack on the World Trade Center in New York City. Obviously, all focus on our local legislative races switched to bigger things. The Primary election was postponed and then re-run two weeks later, but the topics of concern on voters' minds had clearly changed, and a very different campaign picked up from that point.

The haphazard nature of campaigns and unforeseeable circumstances is another reason why the early chapters in this book focused so heavily on understanding your candidacy and your campaign, and building that strong foundation. Things can and will happen that are out of your control, and once the vote is in, it's in.

WINNING, LOSING AND THE FUTURE

About a half-hour after the polls close in your community, you'll start to understand if all of your and your volunteers' hard work has paid off. There are two paths, of course: either you're going to spend the next few years representing the people of your community, or you'll be looking back and asking yourself what more could you have done.

Either way, and although it might not immediately feel like it if you ended up on the losing side, you should be incredibly proud of what you've done. You've taken part in the American political process, putting into action freedoms that our forefathers have fought for to preserve for almost 250 years. You've taken on the responsibility of being a public figure, and you've put your own time, money and energy into forwarding your constituents' agenda. At the same time, you've engaged in what was likely a life-altering process, and learned more about people than you could have possibly imagined – insight and knowledge that you'll be able to utilize in whatever was your original walk of life. Embrace the life experience you've just gone through, no matter what the outcome.

So what's next?

If you've won, we hope that the approach we've offered throughout this book not only gave you the foundation for your winning campaign, but for your time in office. Now, you have the opportunity to fulfill your purpose for running in the first place, but never lose sight of the constituents that got you there. Always listen to what they have to say, and remember that you're their representative in government – a tremendous and time-honored responsibility. In our experience, some of the best re-election campaigns have been run by candidates who continued their grassroots efforts *while* in office, not waiting for the next time the ballots are cast. Walk door-to-door, attend community events and court funders as though the campaign is on – perhaps not with the same intensity, but with the same spirit. And if higher office was your aspiration from the beginning, begin to cultivate the relationships necessary for that leap, while building a resume of effective leadership and results.

For candidates who come up short, if you've followed the advice in this program, you have now built a tremendous foundation for a future run, if you should choose to try again. Losing an election does not mean the end of your political career, but more likely the beginning. You've been through it. You know what you did right, and you know what could've been done better. Because government in America has many local, state and federal jurisdictions, there are other races in your community where you can vie to fulfill your purpose for running, or within a short period of time the race you just finished will be run again. Whatever percentage of the vote you garnered in defeat was that percentage of people who had never voted for you before. What a foundation on which to build! But you know what it took to get that percentage – the toll on your family, your wallet and your feet. You have to weigh that against having caught the "bug" for politics, and determine if you're up for another go at it. We'd predict you're at least thinking about it.

If you choose not to run again, throughout your campaign you've built a network of influential people that may provide another avenue for you to accomplish your goals. If running was a means to an end that positioned you more strongly for action in your community, then your mission has been accomplished. Celebrate that, and enjoy what you are now able to do (without having to worry about 10 p.m. calls to your home phone about a pothole!).

In any case, we wish you the best of luck during your campaign and after, and here's hoping that on Election Night, it's you that's popping the champagne cork.

Looking for more help for your campaign?
How about a campaign in a box?

THE CAMPAIGN COACH'S
COMPLETE CAMPAIGN KIT

Everything you need to run your campaign, including outlines & templates for press releases, scripts, direct mail, get-out-the-vote strategies and much more

Running for office is a lot of work. Let the *Campaign Coach* do the work for you.

ABOUT THE AUTHOR

Craig Turner has worked in government, politics, PR, media and economic development in Western New York for more than 20 years, and is the founder of The Campaign Coach program for local political candidates. Craig is the president of Momentum Public Affairs, a Buffalo-based PR and government affairs firm, and is the author of the WILTON'S GOLD time travel trilogy. He is a graduate of the University of Buffalo, and lives in Wheatfield, New York (near Niagara Falls) with his wife, Nadine, and their four children.

ACKNOWLEDGEMENTS

In 20 years of this business, you learn from a lot of people – far too many to thank here. But there are a few who have specifically played major roles in my journey: Chuck Swanick, from whom I learned more about effective grassroots campaigning than anyone; Bob Davis, who gave me my entrée into local campaigns; Andy Sedita, "Old Pal," who showed me early on that if local politics isn't about people, it isn't about anything; Dave Gallagher, who hired me out of college and let this kid who knew nothing about anything run his newspaper group; and my great friend and mentor, Harry Wahl, who taught me, most importantly, that no matter what happens politically today, you'll still wake up tomorrow and move on to the next thing.

Special thanks to Seth, Bruce, Kristin and Meghan at Market Domination, for helping me turn The Campaign Coach vision into reality.

And to my wife, Nadine, never forgetting that The Campaign Coach concept was her idea.